Jr. Graphic Colonial America

POCAHONTAS AND JOHN SMITH

Andrea P. Smith

PowerKiDS
press.

New York

Published in 2012 by The Rosen Publishing Group, Inc.
29 East 21st Street, New York, NY 10010

First Edition

Editor: Joanne Randolph
Book Design: Planman Technologies
Illustrations: Planman Technologies

Library of Congress Cataloging-in-Publication Data

Smith, Andrea P.
  Pocahontas and John Smith / by Andrea P. Smith. — 1st ed.
     p. cm. — (Jr. graphic Colonial America)
  Includes index.
  ISBN 978-1-4488-5190-4 (library binding) — ISBN 978-1-4488-5218-5 (pbk.) —
  ISBN 978-1-4488-5219-2 (6-pack)
  1. Pocahontas, d. 1617—Juvenile literature. 2. Smith, John, 1580–1631—Juvenile
literature. 3. Jamestown (Va.)—History—Juvenile literature. 4. Jamestown
(Va.)—Biography—Juvenile literature. 5. Virginia—History—Colonial period, ca.
1600–1775—Juvenile literature. 6. Pocahontas, d. 1617—Comic books, strips,
etc. 7. Smith, John, 1580–1631—Comic books, strips, etc. 8. Jamestown
(Va.)—History—Comic books, strips, etc. 9. Jamestown (Va.)—Biography—
Comic books, strips, etc. 10. Virginia—History—Colonial period, ca. 1600–
1775—Comic books, strips, etc. 11. Graphic novels 1. Title.
  E99.P85P57935 2012
  975.5'010922—dc22
  [B]
                                                          2011001708

Manufactured in the United States of America
CPSIA Compliance Information: Batch #PLS1102PK: For Further Information contact Rosen Publishing, New York,
New York at 1-800-237-9932

CONTENTS

MAIN CHARACTERS

Pocahontas (1595–1617) A Powhatan princess. She was also called Matoaka. She became friends with the English **colonists** at Jamestown and helped them. She later married John Rolfe, one of the colonists.

John Smith (1580–1631) An English **explorer**. He was the leader of the Jamestown Colony and wrote about Pocahontas in his book *True Relation*.

Chief Powhatan (?–1618) His given name was Wahunsenacawh. He was chief of the Powhatans and Pocahontas's father. He ruled over the Powhatan empire.

Samuel Argall (1572–1626) English admiral. He kidnapped Pocahontas and held her **hostage**.

John Rolfe (1585–1622) Virginia tobacco planter. He married Pocahontas, and they had a son named Thomas.

POCAHONTAS AND JOHN SMITH

IN 1595, CHIEF POWHATAN AND HIS WIFE HAD A BABY GIRL.

THIS IS MY DEAREST DAUGHTER. I WILL NAME HER MATOAKA.

IT MEANS "SHE ENJOYS PLAYING WITH OTHERS."

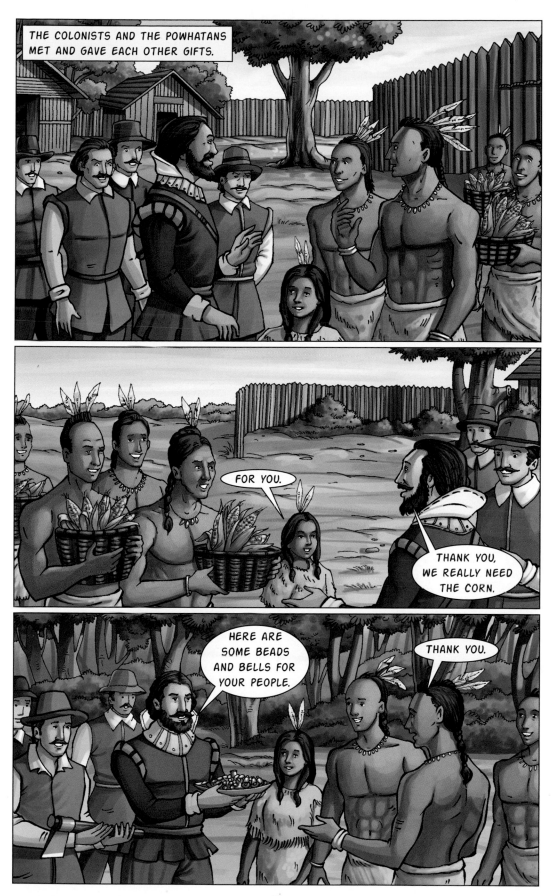

8

14

15

WHILE LIVING IN JAMESTOWN, POCAHONTAS FELL IN LOVE WITH AN ENGLISHMAN NAMED JOHN ROLFE.

POCAHONTAS, I LOVE YOU. WILL YOU MARRY ME?

YES!

IN APRIL 1616, POCAHONTAS MARRIED JOHN ROLFE. HER FATHER DID NOT COME TO THE WEDDING, BUT HE SENT BEAUTIFUL GIFTS.

A YEAR LATER, POCAHONTAS AND JOHN HAD A SON. THEY NAMED HIM THOMAS.

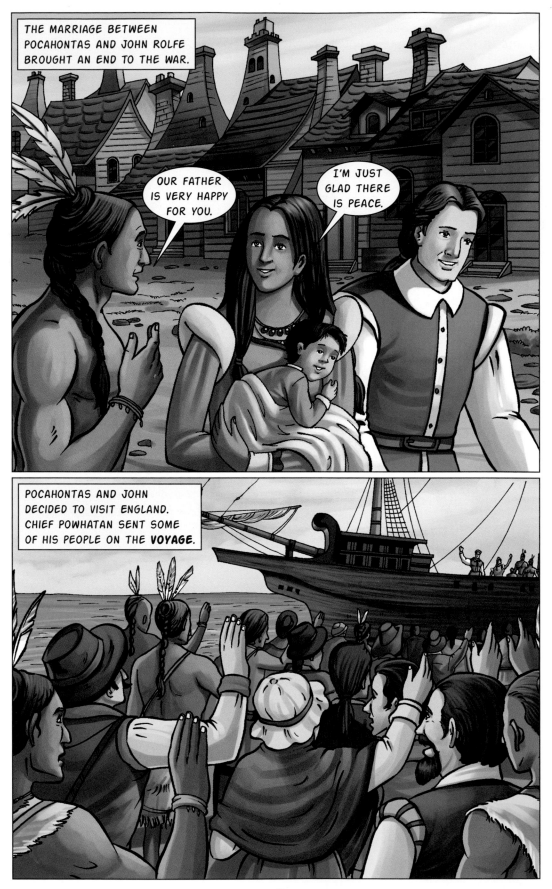

TIMELINE

About 1595   Pocahontas is born.

April 1606   King James I grants the Virginia Company a charter to start a colony in America.

April 1607   The English colonists arrive in Virginia.

May 13, 1607   The colonists begin building Jamestown, on James Island.

June 1607   Powhatan sends word to the colonists that he would like to have peaceful relations with them.

December 1607   John Smith is captured by the Powhatans.

January 1608   The Powhatans let John Smith go.

January 1609   John Smith and his men meet with Powhatan in a Powhatan village. Their trade talks break down, and the colonists leave before Powhatan kills them.

October 4, 1609   After being injured in an explosion, John Smith goes back to England.

1609–1610   Many colonists die of hunger.

1609–1614   The first Anglo-Powhatan War is fought.

1613   Pocahontas is kidnapped by Captain Argall. She is held in Jamestown for a year.

1614   Pocahontas marries John Rolfe.

1616   Pocahontas and John Rolfe travel to England and meet the king and queen.

March 21, 1617   Pocahontas dies. She is buried near St. George's Church, Gravesend, England.

GLOSSARY

baptized (BAP-tyzd) Sprinkled with or immersed in water to show that that person has become a Christian.

captive (KAP-tiv) A person taken by force without his or her permission.

Christian (KRIS-chun) Someone who follows the teachings of Jesus Christ and the Bible.

colonists (KAH-luh-nists) People who move to a new place but are still ruled by the leaders of the country from which they came.

customs (KUS-tumz) Practices common to many people in a place.

explorer (ek-SPLOR-er) A person who travels and looks for new land.

generous (JEH-neh-rus) Happy to give.

hostage (HOS-tij) A person held as a prisoner until some requirement is agreed to.

ritual (RIH-choo-ul) Special actions done for reasons of faith.

spare (SPER) To not hurt or to set free.

swords (SORDZ) Weapons with long, sharp blades.

voyage (VOY-ij) A trip taken, especially by water.

INDEX

WEB SITES

Due to the changing nature of Internet links, Power Kids Press has developed an online list of Web sites related to the subject of this book. This site is updated regularly. Please use this link to access the list:

www.powerkidslinks.com/JGCO/smith